Raise the Bar

The 6-Step Method to Shift from 6-Figure Revenues to 6-Figure Profits in Your Law Firm

Jayden Doyé

Publisher

CHECKMATE PRESS
checkmatepress.com

McLean Media Group, LLC / Checkmate Press
Bozeman, Montana USA
www.McLeanMedia.com

Raising the Bar: The 6-Step Method to Shift from 6-Figure Revenue to 6-Figure Profits in Your Law Firm / Jayden Doyé - - 1st ed.

ISBN 978-1-7321781-6-8

The Publisher has strived to be as accurate and complete as possible in the creation of this book.

This book is not intended for use as a source of legal, business, accounting or financial advice. All readers are advised to seek services of competent professionals in legal, business, accounting, and finance field.

In practical advice books, like anything else in life, there are no guarantees of income or results made. Readers are cautioned to rely on their own judgment about their individual circumstances to act accordingly.

While all attempts have been made to verify information provided in this publication, the Publisher assumes no responsibility for errors, omissions, or contrary interpretation of the subject matter herein. Any perceived slights of specific persons, peoples, or organizations are unintentional.

TABLE OF CONTENTS

INTRODUCTION

My name is Jayden Doye, the Traveling CPA. In this book, you will learn my six-step profit method that helps law firm owners shift from six-figure revenues to six-figure profits without burnout.

I'm going to teach you my six-step method that has successfully worked for several law firm owners.

There's going to be several different topics that will be covered, shifting from one area of law to another area of law, and how to do so profitably.

We will also look at key performance indicators that you need to be aware of in your law firm.

We will address the difference between tax planning and tax preparation.

We will be sure to cover how to organize your law firm so that it can work for you, versus you slaving away working in your business.

This is specifically for law firm owners who have succeeded. You've reached a certain level of success.

However, you're not that happy.

Either you feel like you don't have enough clients, or like you're not serving the right clients, or you're not paying yourself what you truly deserve.

You're not living the lifestyle that you thought you would be living when you first started your firm.

This book is specifically for you if you own your own law firm and take less than eight vacations a year.

The information that you will learn here is very important. As professional service providers, we have normalized burning out. We have normalized 60-hour and 80-hour work weeks.

Truth be told, when you work that long in your business, someone gets the short end of the stick - either your family or your clients. Either way, someone is not being served adequately.

I want to teach others how they can have a business that generates six-figure profits without working 80-hour work weeks. Believe it or not, it is possible, and I will teach you exactly how to do it.

CHAPTER ONE: MY STORY

Before starting my own CPA firm, I had a variety of very interesting experiences in corporate America. For years, I worked several different accounting jobs that I didn't feel served me.

I felt as though I was not challenged, and I did not enjoy working in the private accounting space because the interactions that you have with clients are very limited. You come to work, process, invoice, and go home. That did nothing to inspire me to enjoy my work.

Things changed when I had the chance to join a small CPA firm. I loved it because there was always something new to learn. As a high achiever, I enjoy learning new things.

The feeling of being energized and satisfied in my work quickly subsided once tax season arrived. During this time, we were required to work 50-hour work weeks, or 65-hours if you wanted a bonus.

Oftentimes, I would work these long hours and I would dream about being on a beach. I would just think about all the things I wanted to do, but could not do, because I spent so much time working.

After four years of working at a small CPA firm, I decided it was time for me to start my own firm. And, like many other firm owners, we go into business thinking that now we are going to have freedom, but we get the opposite.

I did not take a single vacation for the first year in business. I was working the same long 50-hour weeks just like I was when I worked in corporate America.

At one point, I worked 80-hours a week for two months in a row. I was so tired… ALL the time. I don't even think I could recognize how exhausted I was.

I could not process the fact that I needed to create systems in my firm, so that I would not be required to work all these hours.

There was no time in my day left to cook. Waffle House food became part of my daily diet. It was during those same two months of 80-hour work weeks that I also gained 23 pounds.

I had gained so much weight so quickly that I developed high blood pressure and high cholesterol. When I went to the doctor, my stats were not favorable. Because the weight came on so quickly, I had to have liposuction to remove it.

After the liposuction, I was forced to stay at home and rest, so I had a lot of time to think about my situation. I thought to myself, 'I'm never going to go through this again'.

Very often when I work with other firm owners, they tell me their goals. They may want to make $50,000 this month, but for that to happen with the current systems in place, they would have to work 80 hours a week. I hate seeing people do that. When you overwork yourself, you can't deliver great quality.

No one wins in this situation.

I wrote this book because I come across so many law firm owners who have high-achieving goals. They want to go on a monthly trip like me, but not at the cost of burn out.

In this book, I will be teaching you the systems I have put into place, for not only myself, but also for other clients, so they can live the life that they truly desire.

My technique is unique because most people either only teach you theory (things that they are not aware of, but they've heard, and they think works) or they teach you strategies that produce great financial results without the balance needed to live a desirable life.

My six-step profit method is a healthy in-between. You can have the numbers that you want in your firm and live the life that you truly desire, with balance.

Most people say, “you can't have it all,” but in this book, I'm going to show you that you can.

I also want to give a special shout-out to my good friend, attorney Andrea Evans. Andrea was a great motivator for me to put this book together. Oftentimes, I’d talk with her about all the things I’ve done to help my clients and she encouraged me to put it into a book. She has held me accountable for over a year now.

Andrea, thank you for holding me accountable.

CHAPTER TWO: COMMON PITFALLS FOR LAW FIRM OWNERS TO AVOID

Most law firm owners know that they need to delegate, but they don't know what to delegate, and to whom. In my profit method, I discuss exactly that.

Hiring is another big topic for law firm owners. Who to hire, when to hire, and what order to hire in. For example, you could hire from the top down or the bottom up, meaning you can start with hiring an associate attorney and then a paralegal, and then an assistant. Or you can do the opposite and start with a virtual assistant, then a paralegal, then an associate attorney.

Depending on how your firm generates revenue and your sales cycle will determine the best way of hiring. It's also important to make sure that you have a sound hiring system. Most people are quick to hire and slow to fire. However, I believe you should be the opposite.

I believe that when hiring, you should have a set of tests, examinations, and tools so you can properly assess if this person would make a good member of your team. You should not rush the hiring process and wait until the last minute when you are in dire need, because at that point, things are likely to only get worse if you bring that person into your firm.

You can't forget about marketing your firm. When it comes to marketing, there's a variety of different methods you could focus on; SEO, social media, direct mail, or network marketing.

One mistake I notice a lot of firm owners make is they spend too much on marketing too early, rather than focusing on organic reach. There are some low-cost methods that are more favorable when you're a small law firm owner when it comes to bringing in your ideal client avatar.

Oftentimes, when I meet with small law firm owners, I show them the return on investment when it comes to their marketing efforts. Often, they are shocked and surprised when I show them the numbers.

It forces them to think about changing their methods so they can not only have more profits in their firm, but they also discover they can pay themselves the salary they deserve for the long hours that they put into the business.

Finally, most methods only address managing a small law firm from one side; either just cash flow, just leadership, just technology, just hiring, just business organization, or just marketing.

My method is a holistic method that addresses all of these topics and will do so from a numbers perspective. And that is what makes my profit method unique.

Most law firm owners avoid working with a CPA because they think they can't afford it or that it's too expensive. But the truth is, you can't afford to not work with a CPA, because there are many shortcomings that they don't know are currently present.

And, if you don't have the right professional to help guide you through those things, then as a law firm owner you could be wasting a lot of money in places that you really don't know.

It's my job to help you become more profitable.

It's my job to help you find those areas to which you're overspending and help you create a strategy to where you can focus your efforts in areas that will increase your profits.

The more money you make, the better it looks for me. So, I have a little bias to make sure that my clients are as successful as possible.

I once helped a law firm owner who focused on family law, business, and bankruptcy. She wasn't happy with the profits that her firm was generating.

When she told me that she focused on three areas of law, I raised my eyebrows. Because usually when a small firm has too many practice areas, that tells me that they are a jack-of-all trades and a master of none. It's hard to look at that person as an industry leader in any one thing.

When working together we uncovered the fact that she did not enjoy working with family law cases, but she did it because she felt like it was more profitable. We moved forward to develop a plan so she could phase out family law and focus on working on bankruptcy.

She wanted to create a firm where she did not have to work too many hours and run back-and-forth to court. She wanted to create a firm that by using technology, she could streamline most of the processes and handle a higher volume of clients.

Her current pricing strategy was underpriced. She was about $1,500 lower than industry standard. By focusing on bankruptcy law, she would be able to double her revenue and profit this year with the strategy I helped her create.

We identified a way to use Google Ads to bring clients in. We then leveraged technology to streamline much of the paperwork process, instead of having to hire another associate attorney to do what a computer can do.

When people start their own firm, if they don't already have a specialty, I usually recommend that they explore the idea of different niche markets.

During my first year of business, I narrowed the niche markets I wanted to serve down to about five or six.

I would create a marketing campaign, run that campaign for 30 days, and then look at the results from that campaign 60 days after that. I spent my first year-and-a-half doing this. During that time, I would also have interviews with people in that market to obtain industry research.

It was during my time interviewing law firm owners where I felt the highest connection. As a licensed professional, I understand the pressure that we have on our shoulders to not only deliver to our clients, but also adhere to the compliance required with the governing bodies that be.

It was in those conversations that I realized there was a need in the market. Very few CPAs specialize in working with law firms because IOTA accounting can be rather difficult.

But, for me, I enjoy puzzles. When someone comes to me and their IOTA account is not up to par and needs to be cleaned up, I enjoy projects like that.

It was then I decided to focus on helping law firm owners because just like them, I understand how difficult it can be to juggle so many things. It made for a perfect type of connection.

CHAPTER THREE: QUIT YOUR JOB AND START YOUR OWN FIRM

The 'P' in the profit framework stands for Proper Planning. A part of that is planning your exit.

There are eight steps I recommend people take to make the shift, whether you currently work at another firm in a traditional nine-to-five environment or work in an area of law that you're looking to get out of and transition into another area.

Step One: Figure out your vision.

Start planning with a trip to the store to get a journal. Block off a few hours every day where you can just allow yourself to dream and imagine.

Different people get inspired in different places. Some people get inspiration in the shower, some people get inspiration in the car. If you're like me, I get inspired at night when I'm laying down. Wherever you get the best inspiration, you want to make sure that you have a method to journal and record those thoughts.

Make sure that you know what your long-term vision is.

- In ten years, what does your life look like?
- Where are you living?
- What kind of lifestyle do you have?

- Are you living on a beachfront property? Are you living in the mountains? Are you living in the city?
- Do you have a spouse? Do you have children?

All these things need to be written down and described in as much detail as possible.

Print pictures that describe your long-term vision. If you see yourself living on the beach in Miami, then you need to go on Zillow or a real estate site to print a picture of a beachfront property. Display it in a place in your home where you can see it - perhaps on your refrigerator.

It needs to be in a central location so every day you can constantly remind yourself what the dream is that you're working towards to create this new reality.

Once we know what the 10-year goal is, it's time to move on.

Step Two: Set specific goals for five years and one year from now.

Break that vision down, because sometimes, the long-term goals are unattainable, so we have to create the halfway market, the five-year goal and the one-year goal.

You want to specifically write down everything that you want to accomplish in five years and what you want to accomplish in one year.

Write it down in the present tense as if you already achieved it. Let's say in five years, you want to be the premier criminal defense attorney for those who are wrongly charged with murder.

You will say, "I am the number one criminal defense attorney within my area for those who are wrongfully charged with murder."

You have to say it in the present tense, and the more that you say it, the more you are telling the universe and the powers that be around you that this is what you want and that is what you will attract.

Step Three: Set the date for when you will quit, or when you will make that full transition.

Set a deadline that you can commit to. I usually recommend a year, because a lot of the business planning process can be done in a year, and that will make the transition much easier.

You also want to tell some of your close friends and family members that can hold you accountable. Do not tell people that are close to you if they are naysayers.

Some people around us do not want us to be successful and because they are so small minded, they will have you doubting yourself. So, only tell this goal and deadline to people that you know will be realistic, but also support you.

Step Four: Create a savings plan.

I recommend having a plan that will allow you to live off that money for six months without any income. Depending on if you plan to have a physical office or not, that can sway your budget one way or another.

You need to create first a budget and then a savings plan so that you'll be okay just in case it takes a few months to generate income.

Step Five: Reduce your workload, if possible.

If you are already working in a firm where you're overworked, then it will be difficult for you to get inspiration, because your energy will be so low.

If possible, you want to either phase out the cases that you don't want to serve anymore if you already own your own firm, or, you want to start taking on less projects if you have an employer. This way you can have the time and energy that you need to commit to the business building process.

Step Six: Start building your business.

Once you have all these ideas, you can start the actual physical business plan. Business plans change, but you need to have one. It doesn't have to be fifty pages. It can be three to five pages, but regardless, you still need a business plan.

Step Seven: Create a list of things as you're getting them done.

Before I started my firm, I bought a big whiteboard. There were so many things that I could not afford to buy at the time. But, as I was able to set money aside, I could purchase the things that I needed and cross them off my whiteboard.

You want to do the same thing for yourself. That way you cannot forget what things you need for you to make the shift.

Step Eight: Have a plan B, plan C and plan D.

Sometimes plan A doesn't work in the timing that we want it to work, which is why you need a plan B, C and D. Let me give you realistic examples.

For me, Plan B was having savings and having a safe budget. That is plan B.

Plan C was my investment portfolio. If things didn't work out and I ran through the savings, I also had an investment portfolio. Now, I avoid withdrawing from my investment portfolio as much as possible, because there are penalties for early withdrawals, so that is why it's plan C.

Plan D could be that, if all else fails, you take 1099 temporary jobs. There are always companies that need some back office and interim support. Start building a list of companies that, if needed, you could do some 1099 work for until your firm generates the revenue that you need for it to be self-sustainable.

As you can see, this plan is solid. If you take those eight steps, then a transition will be a lot easier for you. And remember, I recommend giving yourself at least a one-year timeframe before making that shift.

CHAPTER FOUR: TAX PREPARATION & TAX PLANNING - PROS AND CONS OF EACH ENTITY TYPE

Most people think that tax planning and tax preparation are the same thing, but they are actually very different. When you combine the two, that is how you can maximize your personal and business income investments, even after you pay your taxes.

Let's first define tax planning. Tax planning is creating a strategy to minimize your tax liability legally. We execute strategies and minimize your tax burden. This is a year-round process. It is not something that you do right before your tax return is due.

When you work with the tax planner, they consider current laws, new laws, regulations, and your current situation. The aim is to prepare individuals for the lowest tax liability but keeping them within the current tax regulations.

Now, when we are tax planning for business owners specifically, we have to not only look at where they are today, but where they will be in five years.

When you elect to be in a certain entity type with the IRS, you cannot switch out of it for sixty months. This is where the puzzle pieces come in when it comes to tax planning.

Some of the benefits of tax planning include lowering your tax liability. When you're planning throughout the year, especially when you have business income, this ensures that you take advantage of the right tax credits.

You can use tax loss harvesting techniques with your investments and manage your wealth accordingly. It also ensures estate planning flexibility. Giving money to the next generation is not enough.

Although you may feel great about leaving them money, you may be doing a lot of harm and giving them a complex tax situation. Tax planning not only assures you lower your own tax liability, but the liability of the generations to come after you.

It also helps you understand your investment returns. We live in a digital age. We must deal with the capital gains that deal with crypto, if that's something that you're interested in. Various expenses and even inflation can ruin your carefully-thought-out investment planning, leaving you much less than you anticipated.

For those who are investing in the stock market and digital currencies, it is important to keep your CPA in the loop with your investment activity, so that they may properly advise you.

TAX PREPARATION

Tax preparation is typically a one-time process. Your Certified Public Accountant will prepare your tax return for filing by the tax deadline. Most individuals go through this process between January and April.

Tax preparation requires documents to complete your tax return, including the documentation allocated for your income, such as BW-2s K-1s, 1099s, investment documents, retirement plan statements, and various other documents.

While most people can prepare their tax return on their own, most business owners benefit from having a professional prepare their return for them. One of the benefits being saving more money.

Tax professionals are required to obtain a certain amount of continuing education every year to stay abreast of tax laws and tax compliance. They are usually the ones that can help advise you on maximizing your deductions and tax credits, so that you can keep more money in your pocket.

It also helps you save time. Completing your tax return on your own takes a lot of time and effort. A tax professional can save you upwards of 20 hours. The cost of tax preparation itself can be recouped after just one or two billable hours.

The final benefit is less errors. Having errors on your tax return can delay your refund, but it can also put you at risk for audit and penalties. When you have a tax professional prepare your tax return, this usually guarantees that they follow tax laws and lowers your risk for audit.

Some firms, like Prestige Accounting Solutions, even offer audit protection. We offer $1 million of audit protection for all our tax preparation clients so that, in the event that they are audited, or they receive some types of notices, they know that they have a team that can support them through that process.

TAX PLANNING SERVICES

Tax planners usually offer what's called a tax loss harvesting strategy. If you have a taxable investment account, you can have a large tax liability at tax time. Most recently, we have the big scandal with AMC. I'm sure many people reading this know exactly what I'm talking about. A lot of people made a lot of money from these transactions.

Tax loss harvesting ensures that their investment strategy aligns with the needs of lowering their tax liability. We're working on two things at the same time; maximizing the income that they get from their investments, but also using losses to offset the tax liability that is generated.

Tax planners can also help you to manage your tax bracket. Offsetting certain income can help you minimize how much you owe on taxes. Offsetting may include making retirement plan contributions, or using other tactics so that you can decrease the tax bracket that you're in.

Another service that tax planners offer is managing charitable contributions. In some cases, donating to charity can minimize how much you owe in taxes, and a tax planner can help you determine if that strategy will work best for you.

When it comes to tax preparation, those services usually just include filing your tax returns, ensuring their adherence to federal and state law, managing missed deadlines, and filing the necessary tax resolution paperwork.

One of the essential parts of the tax planning process is ensuring that the business owner is in the right tax entity. Unfortunately, a lot of people avoid working with a CPA who specializes in tax planning, so they do not get the correct advice.

For instance, I helped a client who had their firm set up as a sole proprietorship. We were able to elect that this client be taxed as an S-corporation instead of a sole proprietorship. The fact that we were able to do so in a timely manner allowed us to save this client over $47,000 in taxes.

Sole proprietors not only get taxed at their regular rate, but they also get taxed at another 15.3% self-employment tax on top of that.

Ensuring that business owners are in the right tax entity and, that the election with the IRS is filed timely, is a common service that tax planners offer their clients. Failure to do so can result in the business owner overpaying the IRS.

One of the common mistakes that I see taxpayers make when they file their own tax return is not including all their income. Many times, whether you use a merchant service or work with other businesses, your income is reported to the IRS through Form 1099.

There are times when people forget that they received income from certain people, because it didn't go to their primary bank account.

When leaving out income, it will prompt a 'computer generated audit'. The IRS will send a notice to the business owner saying that they did not report all their income, so they'll be charged tax on the income they forgot, along with penalties and interest of course.

Sometimes the taxpayer did report all their income, but they did not report it in the correct manner. A CPA or tax planner could review that and handle the tax resolution process to ensure that the business owner does not overpay taxes.

Another mistake business owners make is double reporting on their form 1099. Resolving this with the IRS can be a very long-winded process. It involves several different documents to prove that this income was not deposited into the business bank account.

Another common issue when it comes to 1099s is what I call a slide error. Instead of receiving a 1099 for $1,000, the business may receive a 1099 for $10,000. That is a huge difference. It involves not only getting the 1099 corrected by the person that created it, but then also showing that corrected 1099 to the IRS and waiting for them to process it.

TAX DEDUCTIONS

There are several tax deductions you should be aware of in your law firm along with a couple of different strategies you may not have thought about that can help lower your tax liability. Oftentimes, I meet law firm owners who are missing out on many different deductions.

The first strategy is hiring family members. Oftentimes, when professional service providers start making a lot of money, they start having a lot of expenses including putting their kids in the best private schools. Hiring your children is a great way to legally shift some of the taxable income that can be at a higher tax bracket to a lower bracket or shifting it to someone who won't have a tax liability at all.

Let's say your effective tax rate is 25% and your firm pays one of your children $10,000 for administrative duties throughout the year. We have now shifted $10,000 - which would have been taxed as $2,500 if it's at the 25% effective tax rate. We are eliminating that $2,500 by hiring the child.

At what age you can start hiring your kids depends on what state you're in. Every state has different laws as it pertains to hiring children, and you want to make sure that whatever role you hire them for is an actual normal job duty.

You would not pay another person a thousand dollars an hour to make copies. Therefore, in the event of an audit, it would be very difficult to prove that your son who's nine years old is getting paid a thousand dollars an hour. This takes intricate planning in the beginning of the year or the year prior to make this work and have the paperwork in order in the event of an audit.

Another thing people often forget about is time tracking. To provide additional backup in the event of an audit, I recommend time tracking on everyone in the firm. If you were to be audited, you could pull all the time sheets to show when the person was working to support the fee that they are getting.

In addition to hiring your children, you can also consider hiring your spouse. Oftentimes, I've seen clients where their spouse is not working, or they work a low-paying job just for the benefits.

With one of my clients, we developed a strategy where their spouse would be hired as a business development manager in the firm. Instead of them working their teaching job and getting paid $30,000.00, they're now going to get a salary of $100,000.00 from the firm. That salary will be earned by bringing in clients to the firm.

It's a win-win situation. You have someone who is dedicated to bringing clients into your firm, and you have more money that is kept within your household.

Another strategy that you should consider is deferred income. There are a few different ways of deferring income. For example, an attorney fee deferral allows for a contingency fee to be paid in a future year or future period.

As you are deferring these fees, you defer the tax liability that comes along with it. There are two different vehicles to which you can use today for fee deferrals.

One of them is a structured settlement or annuity. It allows you to select payout dates to which your income will come into your firm. You can have that fixed over a fixed period of years or months.

Another option is investment account options. For this you want to talk to your financial advisor to discuss what type of tax deferred accounts would be best for you. You want to make sure that your financial advisor and your CPA are in communication so that your tax plan and your retirement plan are on the same page.

By default, financial planners are usually thinking about gaining the most return on investment in the long term, and CPAs usually think about reducing tax liabilities in the current year.

The best plans that I have found are where both the financial advisor and the CPA can compromise and meet somewhere in the middle to where the long-term goal of the law firm owner having the most amount of money is met.

Another tax deduction that law firm owners should be aware of is meals. If you are taking a client out to dinner, talking to a potential referral partner, or meeting with a prospect, and you're discussing business during that meal, then that meal can be tax deductible.

Since Covid, the government is trying their best to get money back into the restaurant industry. They've changed the law to make business meals 100% tax deductible. Make sure you get a copy of the receipt and write on the top of it who you met with and what the business purpose was. Take a picture of the receipt and if you use an app like QuickBooks, you can easily upload.

In the event of an audit, bank statements will not suffice - they will also require receipts. I recommend all business owners save an electronic copy of all their receipts in their internal files.

Your home office can also be a tax deduction. If you are one of the law firms that is fully virtual and you fully work from home, then there's a chance that a percentage of your home expenses can be deducted for tax purposes - including mortgage interest and insurance, rent, utilities, and renters' insurance.

It's based on how much of the home you use exclusively for business, and you divide that amount by the total square foot of the home.

For example, let's say you have a 300 square foot office in your home and your home is 1200 square feet. 300 divided by 1200 gets you 25%. So that means that 25% of your direct expenses can be attributed to the home office expense.

Be sure to talk to your CPA so that they can help you calculate this for your particular case.

Another expense that oftentimes people forget about are professional fees. Whether it's your accountant, tax preparer, other attorneys, consultants, or coaches, these professional fees that you pay are tax deductible. Working with a certified public accountant is in your best interest because it is tax deductible.

The last one I want to discuss is furniture, computers, and other equipment. If you are someone who likes to sit all day and you don't have a standing desk yet, then consider getting a chair with a back massager.

It is tax deductible because that office chair is exclusively used for business. All of the computers, the equipment, and printers can be tax deductible.

Now, many of these are considered fixed assets. Fixed assets are usually depreciated and not fully expensed in the year of purchase.

What does that mean? The IRS figures if you buy a computer in 2022, you're not only going to be using that computer in 2022, but you'll be also using that computer for a few years. In the IRS code, there are rules regarding depreciating this, meaning we are taking a portion of the expense over the next seven years.

Hypothetically, let's say you buy $7,000 worth of computers, and computers are required to be depreciated over seven years. You will expense a thousand dollars' worth of the computers each year for the next seven years, hypothetically.

Keep in mind, there are ways that you can accelerate depreciation and possibly even take the full expense in the year of purchase, but you have to have a good CPA that knows what they're doing and can protect you in the event of an audit.

The Augusta Rule lets homeowners rent their home for up to 14 days without needing to report the rental income on their individual return. This rule applies to any taxpayer who owns a home here in the United States if your home is not your primary place of business.

The Augusta Rule IRS exemption was lobbied for by residents of Augusta, Georgia in the 1970s. Each year, the Masters Golf Tournament is in Augusta National Golf Club, and the residents of that city wanted to find a way to rent their home to the attendees, so section 280-A was added to the tax code.

Fortunately, today the Augusta Rule not only applies to those in Augusta, but those all over the US. I've seen homeowners rent their home to businesses for either business retreats or business meetings.

Most people think that they can rent their home to their business for $10,000.00 a day for the next 14 days and they won't have to report it on their taxes. That won't work. The rental rate must be market rates, meaning what would other homes in that area or other homes that are of equivalent value to your home rent for each day?

This requires a bit of research. If you can prove in the event of an audit that the fair market rate is $500 a day, then that would be the maximum amount that you should comfortably use if you choose to use the Augusta Rule.

We've come to the time to address my favorite tax deduction. As you all know, I'm all about catching flights and reaching new heights.

Let's consider how you can turn a vacation into a tax deduction. Several different travel expenses to be aware of are the plane, train, bus tickets, baggage fees, laundry and dry cleaning during your trip, rental car costs, hotel, Airbnb costs, business meals and meals that you partake in while traveling to and from your destination.

On a business trip, you can deduct up to 100% of the cost of travel to your destination no matter what mode of transportation you take. Lodging - whether it is Airbnb or a hotel - is also tax deductible. The IRS requires that it's an actual business trip.

So how do we make sure that this is considered a business trip? What I like to tell people to do is to make sure that most of your trip are business days.

Let's say you went to Vegas from Thursday to Tuesday. You fly to Vegas on Thursday. You meet with clients on Friday. Saturday and Sunday are spent zip lining and rock climbing. You meet with clients again on Monday and you fly home on Tuesday.

The IRS does not count Saturday and Sunday - they only look at business days. Out of the four business days you were there, all four would be considered actual business days. Travel days also count as business days.

That's why I usually like to leave on a Thursday so I can get a couple business days in, have a nice fun weekend, and get back to business at the top of the week.

If you bring your family on a business trip, their expenses will not be tax deductible unless they happen to be employees and it's a company retreat for the purpose of growing the bond between all the teammates so that you can increase efficiency and productivity in the firm.

THE PROS & CONS OF EACH ENTITY TYPE

As an attorney, you are probably well-aware of the legal structure of the different entities that you can be in, but it is very important to plan what entity you are going to be from a tax perspective.

SOLE PROPRIETORSHIP

Let's start with the sole proprietorship. This one is the simplest structure to create, and this involves an individual that operates the enterprise. The person is responsible for the business, including all liability and any profit or loss.

Some pros of the sole proprietorship are that it's a good choice for low-risk business. It's easier to start, and tax filing is easy for this. You simply fill out the Schedule C on your individual return, and that is where you put your business income and expenses, and it generates a profit and loss to which you'll be taxed on.

Cons to consider are that it does not produce a separate business entity. Your business assets and liabilities are not separate from your personal assets and liabilities, and you're personally liable for debts and obligations of the business.

Banks are hesitant to lend to sole proprietorships, and the profit on a sole proprietorship will not only be taxed at your normal rate, but also an additional 15.3% self-employment tax.

Usually, a sole proprietorship is beneficial early in the business, but once you start to have a profitable business entity, it does not make that much sense to stay in a sole proprietorship.

GENERAL PARTNERSHIP OR LIMITED PARTNERSHIP

Let's consider a situation in which there's more than one owner. You're either going to be considered a general partnership or a limited partnership.

A general partnership is controlled by two or more businesses or individuals in a partnership. The partners own the company and assume responsibility for the partnership debt and many other obligations.

Pros for a general partnership is that the profits are taxed on the individual basis, not on the business basis. When the Form 1065 is created, that is the tax form for filing a partnership, a form K1 is generated, and that form flows through to the individual return to which the individual pays taxes on that net taxable income.

Partnerships are generally easy to establish. Another pro of having a partnership is that you have multiple people that bring their own skillset to help the business.

Cons of a general partnership are that partners are jointly and individually liable for the actions of other partners, and there's also a self-employment tax that generally must be paid on the net taxable income. When a partner receives a K1, if that flows into their individual return, they will pay their normal tax rate plus a 15.3% self-employment tax rate.

There are ways to avoid that extra self-employment tax rate, but that requires a higher-level tax strategy so I would recommend a CPA set that up for you.

Next up is limited partnerships. A limited partnership is a registered business entity as compared to a general partnership.

Pros of a limited partnership are that limited partners face limited liability for losses, the responsibility of work is duly delegated, and the capital amount in partnership businesses is quite generous.

You have two types of partners in a limited partnership. You have general partners who own, operate, and assume liability for the business, and then you have limited partners - those who act as investors in the business. They are sometimes called silent partners.

Cons of a limited partnership include the fact that general partners bear maximum risk in case of debt. Limited partners are not involved in the decision making so someone could invest a lot of money into a business, but unfortunately cannot make decisions. Based on statistics, the chance of a dispute amongst partners is high.

C-CORPORATIONS

There are then C-Corporations. A C-Corporation is a corporation that is taxed separately from its owners. It gives the owners limited liability, encouraging more risk taking and potential investment.

Pros of having a C-Corp include having the option of splitting profits and losses between the business and the owners to create an overall lower tax rate. You want to check with your CPA on the best way to do this based on your situation.

C-corporations are legally and entirely separate entities from the owners and the shareholders. Owners and shareholders cannot be held responsible for any debt of the C-Corporation, or any lawsuits brought against it. A C-Corporation can sell stock or shares either common or preferred, and there's no limit to the number of shareholders.

Cons include the fact that they face double taxation. The company pays taxes on the corporate tax return based off the net income, and then the shareholders pay taxes on the dividends that they receive.

As a shareholder in a corporation, you will most likely receive dividends based on the profits that the business generated, and dividends are taxable on your personal tax return. Owners, unfortunately, cannot deduct business losses on their personal tax return from a C-Corp, and there are increased regulations and paperwork around operating a C-corporation.

S-CORPORATIONS

Finally, I want to address my favorite, which is the S-Corporation. S-Corporations do not pay income taxes. Rather, the earnings and profits are treated as distributions. The shareholders must receive their income on their individual tax returns.

Here are some pros of an S-corporation; limited liability for management and shareholders, and something called flow-through taxation. Profits from a S-Corp are distributed to the shareholders who are taxed on the profits on a personal level.

There's good privacy and protection, especially in states like Nevada and Wyoming. Oftentimes, when people elect to have their business entity in Nevada or Wyoming because of the legal protection around those companies, they forget that the state that they live in also requires certain reporting to be done.

Even though it may help someone from a legal privacy standpoint, when it comes to taxation, oftentimes it's very difficult to avoid having to pay taxes in your home state or having to report in your home state. When it comes to licensing, that's another thing. If you are only licensed in the state of Georgia, it would not make sense for you to create a firm in the state of Nevada.

An S-Corporation that has two 50/50 partners has a net income of $100,000. If that partnership were a general partnership, then the owners would pay their normal tax rate plus an extra 15.3% tax on that net income. However, with them being in the S-Corporation, when the K1 flows through to their personal tax return, they only pay ordinary taxes on that profit. That would save the partners about $15,000 in taxes if they had a net income of $100,000.

Cons of S-Corps include a maximum of having a hundred shareholders. If you are a high-income shareholder, then the flow-through taxes would not be beneficial for you.

There are limits on issuing stocks with S-Corps versus C-Corps. You can't have more than one class of stock in a S-corporation. Depending on where your profitability will be over the next five years, it's important to plan early on whether the flat tax rate that we currently have on a C-Corporation or the projected tax rate that you have with an S-Corp will be better for you.

Once you elect to be an S-Corporation, to be taxed as an S-Corporation, the IRS will make it rather difficult for you to get out of that for 60 months.

Oftentimes, I get the question, "Can I be an LLC and a S-Corporation?". The answer is yes. The LLC is the legal entity. The S-Corporation is simply your tax entity; how the IRS treats the taxation of the income generated from that business. If you create an LLC and it only has one member/one owner, then by default, the IRS will tax that business like a sole proprietorship.

It's very important that when the business owner creates an EIN, they look at that SS4 letter that they receive. The IRS will tell you exactly when they expect you to file a tax return and by what date that tax return will be due.

They will also let you know if you want to elect to be taxed as a different type of entity, then you need to complete paperwork surrounding that, and that will be indicated on the letter received.

CHAPTER FIVE: THE ORGANIZATIONAL CHART

Having an organized firm is very important because as you grow and scale, you want to know what direction you want to grow in, and what roles need to be hired next. The easiest way to organize the people - the human capital in your firm - is by use of an organizational chart.

An organizational chart is a diagram that shows the hierarchical relationship of job positions within any organization. The most common type of organizational chart is the pyramid style. This shows the CEO at the top and employees below them.

Other types of organizational charts include the matrix style. The matrix style chart has employees working on multiple projects.

In the flat style organizational chart, you'll find no hierarchy. Organizational charts can be used to manage and plan the organization's resources, not only money, but time. As you know in a law firm, tracking time is very important, especially when you bill by the hour. Organizational charts can be used for training and development purposes to show how different jobs relate to each other and identify areas to which improvement is needed.

If you are someone who doesn't like to do a lot of training, you want to make it very clear to new employees of the hierarchy of your firm. Who is the person that they should report to? Who is their direct report? Who are the team members that work directly with them to complete their assignments?

Roles that you need to think of having on your organizational chart include your associate attorneys. Your attorneys will include partners, associates, and contract lawyers. Consider having a legal assistance department. This includes law clerks, paralegals, and legal secretaries.

The next department will be your support staff. This will be your IT support staff, your marketing lead, and your executive secretary. These nine roles that I've named are very important to have in the organizational chart in addition to the chief legal officer.

Too often, I meet firm owners who call themself a CEO - a Chief Everything Officer.

If you want your firm to grow and scale, then you will have to delegate. You cannot do everything and expect your firm to grow rapidly because your time is limited.

Think about it - you have operations, paperwork, licensing, continuing legal education, business development, relationship building, and court.

There are so many different things that must be done. One person cannot do it all and have a large firm.

CHAPTER SIX: STANDARD OPERATING PROCEDURES

It's time to address standard operating procedures.
If your firm has a high turnover and do not have standard operating procedures, I guarantee it will take new hires longer to become equipped to where their performance is proficient

Standard operating procedures are also called SOPs. These are processes that assist with preventing errors. They promote efficiency, and they give a clear direction for employees to complete their task. Every law practice should have SOPs, no exceptions, even if you are a solo firm.

This reduces the risk of inconsistencies, inefficiencies, and unforeseeable mistakes.

Even though it can take time and effort in the beginning, establishing this blueprint for the staff to operate under will increase productivity. It will help your firm spend less time on tasks that they have to do over and over again.

There are seven different SOPs that every law firm should have documented.

SOP #1: SETTING UP CLIENT FILES AND A CLIENT PROFILE

What happens when you obtain a client? Document what forms they need to fill out, what is your standard engagement agreement, all the contact information that needs to be collected, and any contact information for other parties that need to be collected.

You even need to have a standard on how you perform conflict checks. Big firms deal with this quite often but smaller firms, not so much. You may be a small firm today, but years from now that may change. From the beginning, you want to have a procedure regarding conflict checks.

You should also have a procedure regarding how you will set up your initial meeting or meetings. Will they use a link or will your assistant schedule that? Having those things will make it very easy for you to delegate this role of client onboarding to your support team.

SOP #2: RETAINER ACCEPTANCE

I know a lot of people despise having an IOLTA account because it is so much to keep up with. That's what I hear all the time. However, it will make it easy for you, in addition to having legal specific software to help you keep track of not only your IOLTA account, but the subsidiary ledgers associated with it, if you have standard procedures regarding managing this.

Documentation is needed starting with the initial acceptance of the retainer down to closing out the account, correcting errors, and providing a refund. Consider creating a retainer checklist, and you'll have the procedures for the following written down; depositing the funds, reconciling the account, paying your firm invoices from that IOLTA account once you've earned it, making any other necessary withdrawals from the account, and closing the trust account.

All those things need to be properly documented. This will reduce your risk and, as you know, reduce the chance that you'll lose your license for making a simple banking mistake.

SOP #3: INVOICING OR BILLING

This is the one duty that most law firm owners I meet dread the most. I don't know if it's because of the numbers or because it can be tedious, but it's required, of course, if you want to get paid and get paid on time. If you don't have a SOP on this and you don't have a streamline process, it can cause you to close your business.

If the billing doesn't get out on time, then people don't pay on time. If they don't pay on time, then you cannot pay your bills. If you cannot pay your bills, then there is a chance that you will have to close your business. Taking the time to create a billing SOP will be very important.

I would also recommend using a specific legal time tracking and billing system. This will eliminate having to do a lot of the manual work.

I also recommend billing every week. Do not wait until the end of the month to send out bills because your clients might have a lot of bills that they have to pay at the beginning of the month.

Consider creating a standard operating procedure for progress billing. As you are making progress on the different cases, you want to make sure that if their retainer balance is low, that it gets filled within a good amount of time. Don't wait until there's only $5 left.

Based on your firm and your billing practices, find out what the threshold will be. For some people, they will have their clients replenish their retainer when it gets below a thousand dollars. For some people, it's $5,000. It all depends on how money flows in your firm.

SOP #4: MONTHLY REPORTING

For you to grow your practice, you have to know how your firm performs every month. You need to have standard procedures on when you will receive reports, what reports you will receive, how you will review them, and what actions you will take after you have reviewed those reports.

Reports that you want to think about getting are marketing reports. Looking at how much you are spending on Facebook or Google Ads, what that return on investment looks like, and how many leads did you get from that.

On the financial side, you want to consider your profit and loss statement and your balance sheet.

From the operation side, you should look at a report reviewing everyone's time. Where are most of your team members spending most of their time? If cases that you thought would only take 10 billable hours are taking 20 billable hours, then you must think about it.

What is causing the discrepancy? Is it that maybe the client withheld certain information in your initial consultation that then required more work?

Did you not do a good enough analysis upon retaining that client in the first place, meaning you need to make changes to how you go about your initial consultation and your discovery process?

Or is it that the timekeepers that are working on this case need additional training. Maybe they need a checklist to assist them in streamlining their process, but the action that you take will all depend on the reason to which the discrepancy is there in the first place. If you don't have a report, then you won't know the discrepancy.

SOP #5 CLOSING A FILE

When you are done working with a client, how do you properly off-board a client?

- How do you return original documents?
- How will you send a notification that the matter is closed?
- How will you advise the client on next steps to take?
- How will you ask the client to complete satisfaction surveys?
- Do you have a system to ask for referrals?
- How will you send the final invoice?

These are things to think about when creating your client off-boarding or file closing standard operating procedure.

SOP #6: SECURITY PROCEDURES

Solo practices must be very diligent about cybersecurity. There's a lot of valuable and private data in your possession that needs to be protected. Establishing processes to promote security procedures helps small law firms meet their ethical duties.

Now that we are in an environment where we work virtually, what policies and procedures do you have surrounding equipment?

- Is there a document that new employees must sign?
- Are they able to use their own computer and log into a remote desktop or do you provide them with a computer?
- If they get fired, do they keep the computer? Do they return the computer? Your course of action will make the difference between a safe law firm environment and a potential breeding ground for cyber-attacks.

- What is the actual standard software that you will use to protect your system against malware and hackers?

It's your duty to keep all the data private, and you could successfully meet this responsibility with a comprehensive cybersecurity SOP.

SOP #7: VIRTUAL WORK PROCEDURES

Now that many people are working from home, it's important to create procedures around virtual working. For those that do decide to come into the office…

- What requirements do they have?
- Are there hand sanitizers available?
- Do you require a vaccination?

So many different things you have to worry about in regard to protecting your team against COVID-19, but also,

- How do you protect your team from having a computer that's a breeding ground for hackers?
- What are the communication expectations?
- What hours will they work?
- How will they work from home and keep client information confidential?

These are all things to think about as it pertains to creating procedures for a virtual work environment.

CHAPTER SEVEN:
TIME BLOCKING

Effective time management is critical for your business to be successful. I want every law firm owner to understand that the fact that you decided to start your own business proves that you think differently than other people.

You probably get random ideas as you're driving, in the shower or, if you're like me, you get ideas in your sleep. Our brains work differently than people who go to the same coffee shop every morning, get to work at the same exact time, go home at the same exact time, have the same thing for dinner, watch the same show and go to sleep.

It is important that we are clear and purposeful with how we spend our time. When ideas come to you in the middle of the day, it does not mean you stop what you're doing and attend to that distraction. It means you write it down and know that is something you will get to later.

Let's talk about tips that can help you organize your time and organize your business.

First, you have to have a calendar. I have my Outlook calendar, but I also have my Prestige Academy printed planner. On my Outlook calendar, I have different colors to signify different types of activities, so my support team knows exactly what I'm doing, when I'm doing it, and how to help depending on the activity. I have colors designated for current clients, so they know that they must go back the day after and notate my call from that client. I have notes to designate when I'm having a marketing meeting.

There are notes to identify when I'm hosting a webinar. I have a specific color for training and development, so they know they can hop on the call if the topic is something they are looking to learn too.

My morning starts with time in my planner to write down what I'm grateful for. Starting the day with gratitude helps begin my day on the right note.

Next, I write down what I must do for the day. If I see any empty blocks, I fill them because you don't want free time to scroll on your phone and get distracted. Any empty blocks you do have should be used as buffer time or lunchtime.

Create lists of things that you must do this week. Identify a list of long-term tasks. Make a list of ideas that you get and be sure that you prioritize the things that you put on the list.

In my planner, I rank my tasks by A, B, C, and D tasks. The task with the highest priority goes on the A list, and if at the end of the day, I got all my As and Bs done and there's a couple of C things that carry over to the next day, I'm okay with that.

The next step is to time block not only your day, but your week. What day will you focus on networking? People send referrals to people they know, like, and trust, so when are you going to spend time building those relationships? What days will be heavy on client call days?

Are you a morning person, an afternoon person or evening person?

Personally, I don't like to take calls before 10:00 AM, so my system is set up so no one can book a call before then. You might be an early riser. You might be up at 5:00 AM every day, and you want to leave at 3:00 PM. Remember, your firm is customizable. Therefore, you get to create it the way you want.

What day/days of the week will be the days you can cut off all distractions and focus on production? Maybe you have your first cup of coffee at 10:00 AM and from 10:00 AM to 1:00 PM, you defer phone calls and emails and instead, place your focus on reviewing contracts.

This brings me to my next tip; limit your distractions. It's not unusual for many things to pop up throughout the day. It can throw you off from being productive. I always keep my phone on "do not disturb", and my desk phone is only on during my buffer times or where I'm expecting a call.

In your law firm, you should not be the one that's answering the phones all the time. You should have a system in place for someone or a company to answer your phones.

The next tip is to get organized, literally. Did you know that if you have a cluttered office that it can negatively impact your subconscious and can possibly decrease your productivity? Imagine how you feel when you come to a clean office compared to when you come to a cluttered one.

Set aside 5-10 minutes at the end of each day to straighten things up before you leave and scan things that need to be scanned so when you come in the next day, you're coming into a clean office.

My dad always made us clean the house before we went to the store because it was against the rules to leave a house dirty.

Another thing you can do is create shortcuts. Let's say that there are websites that you must go to every day. Have a favorite folder set up for things such as Lexus Nexus and any sites that you use all the time. Have a folder set up so that you and your team can easily access them.

When it comes to emails that you must send periodically, whether that be monthly, quarterly, or daily, make sure that the templates for those emails are saved. Create a template for anything that is recurring in your firm.

Relying on reminders and alerts is such a good help because you could be on a call with a client that's going really well, and if you don't have that reminder, the call will go over.

Once you get that reminder at 1:45 PM that you have another call at 2:00 PM, you know that you must start wrapping up this call, start making any necessary notes, and get it closed out in time for you to get prepped, ready and be on time for your next meeting.

Plan to be early. Try to get on calls five minutes beforehand. Try to get to events fifteen minutes beforehand. Let's say you get to a networking event fifteen minutes early. Now, what's the worst that can happen?

Now you have some extra time to check your emails. Don't wait until the last minute. If you happen to live in a big city like me (in Atlanta), traffic can be unpredictable. One accident could make you 30 minutes late. If you have certain deadlines, do not wait until the day before the deadline to file paperwork. File it early to avoid any last-minute hiccups.

Delegate. You do not have to do every step of every process. When you create a delegation system, you are essentially saying "this person is responsible for steps one through three, this person is responsible for steps four through six, I come in at step seven to review, and then step eight is my responsibility to either deliver to the client or send back for edits."

Make sure that your project or case management system can actually assist you in this process. You should be able to create a profile for everyone in your firm, and for every matter that you have. You should create a workflow. In that workflow, you'll have the different steps of the process.

Let's say you're a trademark attorney. You have different phases of work (for example the research or preparation phase) that don't need to be done by you. You can delegate certain pieces of it to other people. Make a template of that workflow in your system so as soon as you get the payment, it's already assigned.

Another tip is to not overcommit. Oftentimes, it's difficult for people to say "no." Even when they know that they don't have the time and energy, they feel it necessary to help people. If you only have 50% of your energy and you're pretty much running on empty, you're not helping anyone by taking on more than you can handle.

Take this advice. Don't overcommit.

I want you to go into your bathroom today, look in the mirror, and practice saying "no." I want you to say "no" and keep saying "no" until you are completely comfortable saying it. Get it out of your mouth without hesitation. I know it may sound ridiculous, but believe me, it works, and it helps.

The last tip is to make sure that you leave time for self-care. If you don't have time on the weekends to go to the chiropractor, get a massage, get your nails or hair done, or exercise, then incorporate that somewhere in your week. Put it on your calendar like you do every other appointment.

Treat self-care with the same energy that you treat a client appointment. It is important for you to decompress and reset so that you can give your firm the 100% that you need to generate the income that you want to generate.

If you're like me, I incorporate at least four business trips a year and travel to places that I haven't traveled to before. Think about Mexico, Thailand, Japan, Australia. Sometimes a trip to Miami or Dallas just doesn't do it. Or when a trip to DC to look at the nation's capital just doesn’t do it, go somewhere tropical. See an entirely different culture. Go somewhere where the people don't even speak English. You'll be surprised when you experience diverse cultures, the appreciation that you create for what you do have.

If you want to take your computer with you and do some work while you're there, I won't judge you. Just make sure you have some self-care, that you take some time off to reflect and reset while you are there.

CHAPTER EIGHT: AUTOMATION

Legal automation is the process by which you use software to automate your routine tasks. In the 21st century we no longer must do things manually. Computers and technology help us run our firms efficiently.

One of the best benefits of legal automation is that it frees up your time. Without having to manually onboard clients and send routine reminders, you as the owner of the firm can focus more of your time into business development and acquiring high ticket clients.

We like to call that "rain-making." If you want to truly make it rain and be the rainmaker in your firm, then you must use automation to free up some of your time for that.

Automation also helps you reduce the amount of duplication. When you use software to automate routine tasks, it can avoid having two admin team members doing the same task.

For example, let's say that once you obtain a new client, a part of your onboarding process requires you to send that client a questionnaire. If one team member already sends the questionnaire to the client but did not mark that task as completed in your system, then another team member may send the questionnaire again.

Let's say you must draft up some documents for a client. Same situation. The paralegal may see this as something that needs to be done, and another legal team member may see this as something that needs to be done. When your system is not set up to automatically notify the client or notify the team when something is in progress, two people could be doing the same task. That's money down the drain because you've paid someone for labor that did not need to be done.

Automation also helps with a better client experience. Low-value tasks can be automated, and when you're automating these tasks, clients see you as quick on your feet and very diligent. This process of getting onboarded is so easy, it makes them feel even better about working with you.

When you automate, it also helps you have access to data. Automation can save time when doing due diligence, trademark related research, or you have a big contract to review. It helps you reduce the manual time to go through the data while processing more data faster than any human being could.

Finally, it allows you to grow and scale your firm. Using automation allows you to be able to serve more clients in less time. Therefore, this requires less human capital, and less of your manual hours. In this way your revenues severely outweigh your expenses.

Having automation wherever you can, will help your firm get to the multimillion-dollar status sooner rather than later.

LAW FIRM ACCOUNTING SOFTWARE

In addition to automation, you need to have good software. Law firm accounting is unique because you don't only have your general business accounting. General business accounting deals with your general and administrative costs such as rent, when you purchase materials, when you pay for utilities, office supplies, and things of that nature.

When you have actual expenses that are tied to cases, like the direct labor that's tied to cases or when you must pay for professionals to help on cases and you take retainers and that money is put into your IOLTA account, then we also have a higher level of IOLTA accounting, also known as trust accounting.

Unfortunately, some software makes it rather difficult to keep up with your IOLTA accounting. As you likely know, one of the top three reasons why most lawyers lose their license is because of improper use of client funds.

I like to use CosmoLex for any client that takes a retainer. CosmoLex is an all-in-one accounting and legal practice management solution, and it works on the cloud. Now, I don't mean the clouds that produce rain. This is a virtual solution that can be accessed anywhere.

Your accountant can access it from their office and you, and your team can access it from your office. If you have a team that works virtually, they can access it from home. And as you all know, the world is changing as to how we staff our firms. Cloud-based software is really what's trending right now.

Let's talk about some of the pros of all-in-one software. CosmoLex has a built-in accounting suite. It does not necessarily require you to have QuickBooks. Most practice management solutions for law firms do not have a built-in accounting suite. Sometimes the integration with QuickBooks doesn’t work and it makes it much harder for the accountant.

With CosmoLex, you get free unlimited training and customer support. You can accept online payments with LawPay, and you have a free login for your external accountant, so you don't have to pay for that user. It's cloud-based, so it can be accessed from anywhere.

Check printing is very easy if you still print checks and there is flexibility to integrate this with other software to import your billing. It also has parameters in place so that you cannot go negative in your IOLTA account.

Now, here are some of the cons of this software. Unfortunately, it does not have an integrated payroll system. They have tiered pricing, but it's only available for firms that have 10 or more users.

There's multiple line data entry which means that when you're adding up multiple expenses manually, users say that the load time can be a little laggy for entering multiple expense items on invoices.

How do you know when it's time to change software? It really comes down to time and money. Consider if you feel like there is a task or several tasks that you are performing in your firm and it's something that you do on a regular basis.

If your software does not have any type of automation feature to assist you in streamlining this process but something else does, you want to compare the savings that you'll get from the labor expense to the cost of the software.

Let's say this software costs $75 a month/$900 a year and it will save you five hours a week, and let's say the labor expense allocated to those five hours is $50 an hour. Per month, you will be saving $1,000 of labor cost. For the whole year, you'll save $12,000 of labor cost and the software only costs $900. There is a net benefit of $11,100.

You also want to think about the time and effort it will take to switch over. There is some software in which change management can be a smooth process where the software provider assists. If that takes, let's just say, 100 billable hours, you want to make sure with this low-value expense that you don't have the person in your firm with the highest labor expense responsible for the switch over.

In the end that will cost you more than it will save you. Let's say you had an admin person who could take care of the switch over, and you paid that person $20 an hour. If it took 100 hours for implementation, the total cost of implementation would be $2,000. In our earlier example, we already had a net benefit of $11,100. So, if we subtract $2,000 from that, we're still at a net benefit of $9,100.

You also want to consider if you will need to upgrade to a higher level in the future. Let's say after five months, this software is working so well that now you've acquired so many clients and you're at the max of the tier pricing.

Now, instead of $75 a month, you must pay $100 a month. When we budgeted $900 earlier for a whole year, now we must allocate an additional $25 a month for seven months. No biggie, that's only an extra $175. For this example, in the end, we still have a net benefit of $8,925. If there's software out there that can either do what humans do or streamline the work that humans in your firm do, then if you can afford it and if the net benefit is much higher than the cost, consider making a switch.

I once had a client who would use spreadsheets to keep track of their IOLTA accounts and client billings, and they were doing billing on Microsoft Word invoices.
I told them they needed time entries and billing to be all in one software, so they needed to streamline the process. This lawyer had a billable rate of $5,000 and they were spending about 12 hours a month with this manual process. So that's about $6,000 in labor costs to the billing process.

We were then able to take that down to one billable hour per week. It went from 12 hours down to only four hours a month. We saved them eight hours per month by switching software.

We've now saved this person $4,000 a month and the cost is only going to be an extra $75 a month because all of their time, entries, their billing, their client communications, the client portal, and all the direct expenses to cases are all put in one system. That streamlined what they were able to do and now they're bringing on a higher caseload than they were before they worked with me.

Truly, the benefit is much higher than the $4,000 that we found.

CHAPTER NINE: FINANCIAL STATEMENTS

The core three financial statements that every law firm owner should be aware of and view monthly are the income statement, the balance sheet, and the cash flow statement, also known as the statement of cash flows.

THE BALANCE SHEET

The balance sheet shows the company's assets, liabilities, and equity at a certain point in time. At the top, you'll see the asset section. This starts with the cash and cash equivalence, and it will show the balance and ending cash at the time of the statement. For example, let's say your balance sheet is dated December 31st, it will show how much cash you had on December 31st.

Then, under the assets, you'll see liabilities. This shows what you owe other people. Typical liabilities will include your credit cards, a car loan, and things of that nature.

Last but not least, you'll see your equity account. This shows how much equity you have or if you have other shareholders, how much equity all the shareholders have in the business.

The key feature of the balance sheet is that it shows the financial position of a business. It shows a snapshot of the financial picture of the company at a specific point in time.

Remember this equation; assets = liability + shareholders' equity. When you're looking at your balance sheet, you want to be aware of whether your assets are higher than your liabilities.

If you only have $2,000 in the bank, but you have debts of over $200,000, when it comes to lending, companies will not look at your business as a healthy business.

There will be periods of time when your liabilities will be much higher than your assets e.g., when you have just acquired a business loan. However, that should not be normal. It can make sense for that to happen during certain periods of time, but it should not be the norm.

THE INCOME STATEMENT

The income statement starts at the top with your income accounts. It will show things such as your legal fee income, reimbursable income, product income if you sell products, and cost of goods or cost of service. If you have products, then the cost of those products will be there.

If your accountant considers your labor cost to be a cost of service, then your labor will go directly in there as well. When you subtract your gross income from your cost of goods or cost of service, you have what's called "gross profit".

From there, next is shown the operating expenses. The operating expenses are deducted from your gross profit, and this gives you the bottom line, your net income.

Some key features that you should be aware of in the income statement is that it shows the revenue and expenses of your business over a period of time. You could show this statement for a year, a quarter, or a month. There are so many different periods to which you can show your income statement.

If you want to view your income statement as you progress through the year, you want the income statements set up to display next to each other so you can view where things are going.

Is the trend of the income going up, or is the trend of the income going down? Are there certain expenses that seem to be more sporadic? Are there certain expenses that seem to be too high as compared to your income? Are your expenses and income in line with the projections and the budget that you set forth? These are all things that you need to consider.

Your income statement is used to assess your profitability, and that's why we're all here - to increase our profits. To increase your profits, you first have to know where your business stands as far as profitability. To do so, you'll need to examine your income statement every month.

THE CASH FLOW STATEMENT

The cash flow statement is used to answer the question; where did all your money go? It will show you the increase and decrease in cash over a certain period. It has three sections: cash from operations, cash used in investing, and cash from financing.

It starts out with your beginning cash, and then what's either added or subtracted is your cash from operations, also known as your net income. What's shown is the cash that was either used or that came in from investing in financing activities.

If you used credit cards or got a loan, or if the owner contributed money to the business or took out distribution, it will all show on your cash flow statement. Believe it or not, it is possible for your bank balance to barely move from month to month, but for you to still show a net income.

For example, there may be a month where you weren't even able to pay yourself, so you don't see how you had a profit that month. Instead, you took a lot of cash and you put it towards those loans that you signed up for.

You personally didn't see any of the cash, but it was there. You did generate a profit and it went to pay off a loan, which is why it's so important to be very strategic when you borrow money for your business.

A good software like CosmoLex or QuickBooks will be able to provide you with the financial statements that you need to view from month to month and assess the health of your business.

COMMON MISTAKES TO AVOID WITH FINANCIAL STATEMENTS

When people are selecting an accountant it's not unusual that they want to choose to work with the one who is cheapest. There's a reason why certain accountants are cheap. It's because they don't know what they're doing.

It's not uncommon that when I look at financial statements, I see improper categorization. For example, when you pay a car note, you don't create an account called "car loan expense." The payment goes to reduce the liability.

A portion of that payment may be expensed in the form of interest expense, but you would not create an expense account to pay off a liability. That is the number one mistake that I see on financial statements.

Another mistake that I see is the bank account has not been reconciled. At the end of every month, the bank account is reconciled in the accounting system to verify that everything in the accounting system matches what is on the bank statement.

Sometimes there's certain activity that you don't see until the reconciliation process. Those can include bank fees, interest that was put on the bank account, and uncleared checks. All of that is handled during the reconciliation process.

It's not unusual to find people who go the whole year without reconciling. When they try to reconcile at the end of the year, they see there's a difference and they just throw the difference over to what's called "reconciliation discrepancies". This is an expense account in QuickBooks.

I have seen some large balances and reconciliation discrepancies that should never be used. If the bank account has not been reconciled, that means that all the activity is not correct. Therefore, you have improper financial statements, and you cannot make data-driven decisions.

This is a prime reason that every step of the process has to be done correctly. This really speaks to the importance of having the right person processing the bookkeeping for your firm.

KEY PERFORMANCE INDICATORS

In business, key performance indicators are essential for measuring progress and determining whether you're meeting your goals. For law firms specifically, common KPIs include billable hours, new client acquisitions and cases won.

Additionally, KPIs can help law firms to set realistic goals and benchmark their progress over time. Ultimately, using KPIs is one of the best ways to ensure that your law firm is operating at the highest level of efficiency.

Law firms are under constant pressure to perform. They need to maintain a high standard of legal services while also ensuring that they're profitable. Like any other business, law firms can use KPIs to assess and improve their overall performance.

While client satisfaction is obviously important, it can be difficult to accurately measure. This is because law firms often have a wide range of clients with different needs and expectations. What one client considers to be satisfactory may not be the same as other client expectations.

Additionally, law firms typically have long-term relationships with their clients, so measuring client satisfaction can be a challenge. Despite these difficulties, law firms must still strive to provide the best possible service to their clients and use surveys to document their satisfaction rates.

It is also important to always look for ways to improve and measure the success of your marketing efforts. One important metric is the number of new inquiries generated by marketing activities. This can be tracked by keeping tabs on the number of new phone calls, emails, and online form submissions received each month.

Another important KPI is the number of new clients acquired because of marketing activity. This could be tracked by monitoring the number or percentage of inquiries that ultimately result in paying clients.

Finally, law firms should track the return on investment of their marketing spend by calculating how much revenue is generated for every dollar that's invested in marketing. I recommend law firms use a KPI tracking spreadsheet to keep track of their marketing efforts.

In addition to marketing KPIs, there are some financial KPIs that can help law firms keep track of their progress in several different areas. These areas include revenue growth, cost containment and profitability.

By monitoring these KPIs on a regular basis, law firms can identify and address problems early on before they have a chance to impact their bottom line. In today's competitive legal market, any advantage that law firms can gain from tracking their financial KPIs can be the difference between success and failure.

Two other KPIs that law firms should be aware of is the churn rate of employees and clients.

Some law firms have normalized the idea of a client only working with them for a short period of time and then moving on. For example, let's say you're a family law attorney. Once you do the divorce for a client, they may not need you for another five years.
Hopefully in their mind, they won't ever need you again, but realistically, things happen. For every client that you lose when you have closed the case, you need to be intentional to bring on new clients to supplement the income that you will no longer get from the client that you're off-boarding.

In addition to keeping up your client count, you want to make sure that you are not constantly losing employees. If employees quit every 90 days, that may be an indicator that there needs to be an improvement on the environment that you are creating for your firm.

Why is it that people are quitting? Realistically, when they give you their two-week notice, they will most likely give you a blanket response, like they are seeking opportunities elsewhere. What they won't tell you is that there's low project management, low company morale, it's not fun to work there, and they don't feel valued. Those things are very difficult to get out of someone that's leaving.

You want to make sure that several times a year, you ask your employees to complete an anonymous survey so they can give their true feelings on what it feels like to work with you, thus reducing your employee turnover rate. When you have an employee that quits and then you must hire a new person, there is a level of cost that comes along with that learning curve.

There's an extra cost that comes along with that person having to learn your systems, processes, procedures, software, and things of that nature. It's in your best interest to be able to keep employees for the long haul.

CHAPTER TEN: IOLTA ACCOUNTING

The IOLTA account is the least favorite topic that law firm owners come across. It's a type of trust account that can collect interest, and those interests are usually transferred out for the state bar or charitable purposes for the provision of civil legal services for people that need services at a free or low cost.

Every state has certain parameters surrounding IOLTA accounts. However, I will discuss the general rules that apply to an IOLTA account. Many people have difficulty understanding this concept so I will be breaking it down so that all law firm owners can truly understand it without difficulty.

The biggest difference between a law practice and any other business is that there are operating accounts and trust accounts. When a firm receives a retainer and that money is not earned, that money must go into the trust account.

In this chapter, I will be using trust account and IOLTA account interchangeably. However, for that bank account, if there are any fees that come out of the operating account, they do not come out of the trust account.

The law firm must, according to their cash management, transfer the money when earned from the trust account to the operating account.

HANDLING RETAINERS PROPERLY

Money that you've received, but not yet earned, goes into the IOLTA account. Whether you prepare your bills monthly or weekly, you will list your fees and costs associated with the matter.

For example, you have a $5,000 retainer for a client, and let's say you do your billing on the 15th of the month. This means the activity from the 1st to the 14th includes billable hours in the amount of $2,000. On the 15th, you'll bill your client $2,000. Now that the bill has been sent, you can now move the money from the IOLTA account to your operating account because you have now earned $2,000 from billable hours.

Let's say it's time to pay rent. It's the first of the month. Rent is $2,000, but you only have $1,000 in your operating account. If you are thinking about transferring the money from the IOLTA account to cover that rent and you promise you'll put it back, you need to disregard that thought right now. You cannot pay operating expenses out of your IOLTA account. This money is not really your money.

What you do is you transfer the money from the IOLTA to the operating once earned, but do not pay operating expenses out of your IOLTA account. That will get you into hot water with the bar.

You want to make sure that you keep good records. There are strict record keeping requirements when it comes to having an IOLTA account. You need to have a separate ledger for every client that you've had funds for in that account. You need to have copies of invoices, bills, check images, and I usually recommend having some type of reconciliation sheet for each matter.

A THREE-WAY RECONCILIATION REPORT

Depending on which software you're using, oftentimes the software will do most of the work for you. However, if you're not using an up-to-date legal management software that has an accounting feature in it, it will be difficult for you to create what's called a "three-way reconciliation report."

Many bar associations require that you have a three-way reconciliation report. This report shows that your bank account balance, your book balance, and your balance by matter all equal up.

They want to make sure that your accounting system, your records, and your bank statements are all in line and that you are not misappropriating funds.

Let's really break down what each one of these terms mean as it pertains to bank account balance, book balance, and balance by matter.

BANK ACCOUNT BALANCE

Your bank account balance is the amount that's shown on the bank statement. If there are any errors, they should be reported to the bank and addressed immediately. Failure to report an error in a timely fashion can remove the obligation of the bank to fix it. Being intentional about checking your bank account can also help you stop fraud.

Ideally, the bank returns and clears checks and copies of checks. These can be readily available using online banking. If there are old unclear transactions, those should be handled in the manner designated by your bar association. This usually means finding the person that is owed the money or returning funds to a client.

If that can't be done, you must turn the funds over to your state. States have rules about how long you can wait on these older transactions, so make sure you know your state's guidelines.

BOOK BALANCE

Book balance is the amount that you show for the IOLTA account on your financial statement. The balance sheet will reflect the IOLTA bank account, and you'll also have an associated liability account on your balance sheet.

Since the IOLTA account is not money that belongs to the firm, there should always be a liability account with the balance matching that of the bank account. This will properly reflect the positive and negative, so the values are not part of the firm's value.

The book balance may not match the bank balance, and that's only because of uncleared checks or deposits. These may have older items that haven't been handled or transactions that have not had time to pass through the bank clearing system. The book balance should equal the bank account balance adjusted for unclear transactions.

When you reconcile a bank account in your accounting software, there is a portion of the financial statements where it shows the adjusted balance of your bank accounts that attributes for all your unclear transactions. If you are confused about where you can view transactions that haven't cleared yet, your bank reconciliation report is where you can find them, providing you put all your transactions into your system as they occur.

BALANCE BY MATTER

The third term to be aware of is balance by matter. This is a list of how much money is in an IOLTA account that belongs to each matter or client. This should match the book balance. If it does not, you need to know why.

There are two main discrepancies that can be avoided. First, the IOLTA interest deposited one month and removed from the next can throw off the balance. Second, firm funds deposited into the IOLTA account to handle fees shouldn't be taken out of that account. To avoid these discrepancies, make sure that you have a standard operating procedure for tracking client funds.

This is the reason why I recommend billing processes be done weekly versus monthly because it forces you to look at your balance by matter and by client and it can help you catch any discrepancies sooner rather than later. If you follow these rules, this will minimize the risk of co-mingling funds and losing your license.

I love using CosmoLex because it makes it impossible to go negative in an IOLTA account in your accounting system. It has parameters in place to help the law firm owner easily trace IOLTA account funds. Many times, my attorney clients work on different matters for a client.

For example, a business attorney may start out with a business formation matter for a client, and they will have leftover funds in their IOLTA account. Eventually, that client needs contracts done. Once another matter is created, the funds from the closed-out matter are transferred to the new matter.

In this case we started with a balance of $5,000. After the formation, it went down to $3,000. After the contracts are done, maybe there's a dispute that they must handle. We spent S1,000 on the contracts and now the $2,000 goes to the next matter, which will be the dispute.

Let's say the dispute requires the full $2,000 remaining. At that point the system and CosmoLex can show you how and when the funds were transferred, as they were transferred from the IOLTA to the operating account. You can also see when they were billed and as they were transferred from one matter to the next. I love

QuickBooks, but unfortunately QuickBooks does not do that.

CHAPTER ELEVEN: MONEY MANAGEMENT & PROFIT GROWING TIPS

In this chapter, I'll address a new cash flow method that will assist firms in ensuring that their firm is profitable. It will get them in tip top shape as it pertains to cash flow management.

Oftentimes, firm owners only have about one, two, or three bank accounts. I see they have a checking account, a savings account, and if they take a retainer, an IOLTA account, also known as a trust account. I recommend that you have a minimum of four to five bank accounts.

THE INCOME ACCOUNT

First, we will start with the income account. This should be a checking account to which all your earned income will go into. If you bill a client and they have a retainer and you shift money from the IOLTA account, all that money will go into the income account as earned income.

If you have a subscription service and you need to figure out which account that money should go into, all of it should go into the income account. You will distribute money from that income account twice a month following the percentages I recommend on the 15th and the last day of the month.

THE OPERATING EXPENSE ACCOUNT

You will have another checking account called your operating expense account. This account is what you'll use to pay your day-to-day business expenses, payroll, etcetera. You will only put a maximum of 70% of your income into this operating expense account.

THE PROFIT ACCOUNT

Next, you transfer 10% into your profit account. This will be a savings account, and this account will be used for the owner to take quarterly vacations. It can also serve as your firm's rainy-day fund, and you will only draw on it in dire situations. If your firm needs to temporarily supplement cash flow, you have it there.

But you want to make sure that you're saving it there for those quarterly vacations. When you can reset, refresh, and reflect on what worked and what didn't work the previous quarter, you'll be able to go into the new quarter with a fresh mind.

THE TAX SAVINGS ACCOUNT

Lastly will be your tax savings account. Depending on how much revenue your firm is generating, I usually recommend 10% to 20% into this account. This is another savings account that will be used for your business and personal income taxes. What often happens if it ends up being too much savings, you now have extra money to put towards big investments into the firm.

Think about those times where you wanted to buy a series of computers. Perhaps you needed to drop $5,000 for computers, or you needed to have $10,000 for an investment to work with a professional service provider and you didn't have it.

By overfunding this tax account, it serves not only to make sure that you always have the money for your quarterly estimated tax payments, but it also serves as a long-term savings account for those big investments that you want to make for your firm.

To recap, you will have your income account where all your earned income will go into and twice a month, on the 15th and the last day of the month, you will empty that income account and distribute those funds to your operating expense account at 70%, your profit account at 10%, and your tax savings account at 20%.

Now, I know that you're probably thinking that right now that might be difficult for you to do, because you are just keeping your head above water. Maybe your operating expense right now is 90% of income. You need to figure out what you can do to cut back on expenses so that you may increase your firm's profitability.

MAXIMIZING YOUR FIRM'S PROFITABILITY BY CUTTING EXPENSES

This is my favorite tip on how to maximize your firm's profitability by cutting expenses - avoid bad clients. Think of those times where you had a consultation with the client and you were saying to yourself, "Man, this person is a lot." Deep down inside you knew that this person was not going to be a good client, but you thought you needed the money, so you took them anyway.

These headaches are oftentimes causing a bottleneck in our firm. Oftentimes, these are the ones that want to pay the least and want the most. Those types of clients should be avoided.

Starting today, have a rubric that you use when it comes to working with new clients. You need to make sure that there are certain things that you will tolerate and will not tolerate as it pertains to bringing in new clients. Even when the money sounds great, sometimes it's not worth the headache.

Another tip is to raise your rates. A lot of times people hesitate to raise their rates. However, over the past few years between the pandemic and inflation, we've seen rate increase across several different products and services. If you have not raised your fees in the past two years, I am giving you permission today to raise your rates.

It will take some market research on your side to determine how much you should raise your rates. You also must consider if you are going to be the luxury end of the market, or are you going to be the cheap end of the market? Do you want to be more like Gucci, more like Walmart, or do you want to be in the middle?

If you're a small law firm, I don’t recommend that you come in being cheap, because cheap only works if your firm does a large volume of work. To obtain a large volume of clients, it takes a very, very large marketing budget.

Many small firms do not have the capital to support a marketing budget that these large volume firms have. This is where you can think about how you bring something unique to the market, and what does that specific niche look like as far as clients are concerned, that are willing to pay a premium for you to solve their problem?

Always make sure that you're billing accurately and often. Many times, I meet firm owners who only deal with billing once a week or once a month rather, and the failure of billing often is actually causing the firm to miss out on money and slows down cash flow.

Make sure that you're asking for client feedback. Clients may not be comfortable telling you what issues they have or where your firm can improve, and maybe that person could be a repeat client if you could rectify issues.

Asking for client feedback will ensure that your performance is in tip top shape, and that your clients will continue to come to you to solve their legal issues.

You want to make sure that you're double checking your expenses at least monthly. Sometimes there are subscriptions that we continue to pay but we don't use and because we don't double check our expenses, we end up paying for them for months - or worse, years - without using them. Make sure that you're double checking your expenses.

You also want to make sure that billing from all your vendors has been done correctly. Sometimes companies may double bill you or maybe they billed you an incorrect amount. You want to make sure that all the amounts that you're paying are correct.

Have the option for your clients to pay in full or pay in advance. Most times people feel uncomfortable asking for a large sum of money upfront. Let's be realistic! If you know that the case will cost $10,000, then you can just let them know that you'll take $10,000 today.

Don't automatically assume that the client will not have the money to pay you in full upfront. Sometimes they will. Sometimes they will need a payment plan. Let the client tell you that they need a payment plan. Don't automatically tell them that there are payment plan options.

When it comes to cutting costs specifically, look at your staffing expenses. You want to look at the cost that you pay your staff and divide it by your income and use that to determine if your labor rate is a favorable rate. A rule of thumb is that your firm's labor rate should never go above 30%. This does not include the salary of the owner.

Depending on where you are in your business - if you just started, if you're growing your firm, if you have a $100,000 firm versus a million-dollar firm - these numbers can fluctuate.

The benchmarks change based on what industry of law you're in as well. Often, firms are very heavy on labor expenses. This is why it's also important to track time. If you look at the time that your team puts into each case versus the revenue that you are obtaining per case, you can better determine if you need to reduce staff or maybe if your staff needs more training so that they can be more productive.

You also want to look at your actual physical space needs. A lot of firms are overpaying for large offices just to have an image of being a prestige firm. Now that we work and live in a digital age, a lot of firms are going virtual, and your clients will actually never come into your office.

Instead of paying that $5,000 a month for that fancy space on Peachtree Road in Atlanta, consider using a service where you only pay for the office when you use it. There are many different services out there where you pay a monthly fixed rate for the subscription.

If you need to use a conference room or need to use a private office, then you can pay additional fees. Many times, for firms that are mainly remote, this option is very cost saving for the firm.

Also, you want to look at your different vendor arrangements. Look to see if your vendors may have some type of options where you can either prolong payments or split payments.

For example, if you're buying equipment, maybe that vendor has an option where you can pay them Net 30, meaning you do not have to pay in full today. You can pay the full balance within 30 days. This will give you some additional time on your cash flow.

Let's consider if you have an excess of cash, but you're looking to save on expenses. You may even consider paying full options for your vendors. Many times, professional service providers provide a discount or some type of incentive if you pay for the subscription in full upfront, rather than doing monthly payments. If you signed a 12-month contract and you know that you will pay for the service for the next 12 months, then it may benefit you to pay in full if it will not negatively impact your cash flow too much.

Finally, lawyers are known for negotiating contracts and various things, so use that skill set when it comes to paying your vendors. Oftentimes, if a service provider does not have a pay in full discount, don't hesitate to ask them if they are willing to give you a

10% discount if you were to pay this full contract upfront.

If you are going to pay somebody $30,000, I'm pretty sure that they will be willing to consider giving you a $3,000 discount to get the full payment upfront. But if you don't ask, you shall not receive.

REVENUE GOAL SETTING

When I ask firm owners how much they want to make. They stare back at me confused for a minute and then start pulling numbers out of the air. This is when you need to think about SMART revenue goals.

I'm pretty sure you have all heard this acronym a thousand times. SMART stands for specific, measurable, attainable, relevant, and time bound. A good example of a SMART goal would be to increase revenue by $50,000 by December 31st, 2023.

As you can see, it's very specific. It's measurable. An extra $50,000 is attainable. It's relevant to business, and by giving it a deadline it is time-bound. When setting your revenue focused goal, there are some things you'll want to consider. It's not only the number, but the story behind the number.

You must think about the actual cost per lead. You could say that you want $50,000, but on average, how many clients will it take for you to get to that $50,000? You first must look at the average value per case. This is extremely important.

Once you have your average value per case, you can back that into the number to get the goal of how many new clients you need. For example, let's say your average value per case is $5,000. Your revenue goal is $50,000. You know that you need 10 more clients to get to that goal.

Now that you know how many clients you want, you must figure out what strategy you'll use and what it will cost to obtain those clients.

You need to look at your KPIs as it pertains to marketing. You want to look at how many leads you've generated over the past year, and how many of those leads have converted over to clients. This will give you your conversion rates.

Hypothetically, let's say you had 1,000 leads, and of those 1,000 leads, only 50 of them became clients. That means your conversion rate is 5%. So now you know your conversion rate and you know how many clients you need. You need 100 clients, and your conversion rate is only 5%. You divide the two numbers. You divide the clients that you need, in this example 100, and your conversion rate of 5%.

Based off the historical data, you will need 2000 leads in order to meet this revenue goal. Now that you know how many leads you need, you need to make sure that we have the money to obtain these leads. The next number that you need to get is your cost per lead.

To get this number, what you will do is you will take your total marketing costs over the past year and divide that by the number of leads that you have generated over the past year. Let's just say hypothetically, last year you spent $10,000 on marketing, and that got you 1,000 leads. When you divide the total of 10,000 by those 1000 leads, you get $10.

That is your cost per lead. Now you multiply that cost per lead times the number of leads that you need, which in this example is 2000, and you get a total of $20,000. We know that we need to budget $20,000 to obtain these leads that we need to meet this new revenue goal.

Now, keep in mind that over time, realistically, our marketing efforts should increase. Meaning if we used marketing efforts last year, we should have done some type of analysis to figure out what works and what doesn't work. Every year, your cost per lead and your cost per clients should decrease because you should analyze to see what is converting people over.

Sometimes I see lawyers who have a link to free consultations or free webinars, and sometimes that works and sometimes it does not. But you really must make sure that every new client that comes in, you know where they came from. This will help you in your efforts to ensure that you are not over expending marketing so that you can truly maximize your marketing dollars.

FINDING YOUR TARGET MARKET

Too often, I go to a law firm owner's website, and it says they can help anybody that owns a business with contracts. Casting a wide net doesn't necessarily work in your favor as far as catching the best fish.

How do you make sure that you target a specific market to catch those big fish that you're looking for?

Let's first start by looking at what a niche market is and why you need one for your law firm. At its most basic, a niche market is a group of potential clients with a shared goal or need.

For law firms, this can be anything from divorce law to patent law. By focusing on a specific area, you can develop expertise that will make you more appealing to potential clients.

In addition, niche markets tend to be less competitive than the broader legal market, making it easier to stand out of the crowd. Finally, by targeting a specific market, you can better tailor your marketing efforts to reach your ideal clients and truly find those big fish.

In today's saturated marketplace, having a niche market is essential for every law firm that wants to succeed. Now, I know you're wondering how to find a niche that works for you. Well, there are many factors to consider, including your area of expertise, your target clientele, and your marketing strategy.

One way to get started is to talk to other law firm owners or partners about their experience. Ask them what niche markets they have targeted and why they choose those markets. You can also look for articles and blogs about choosing a niche market for your law firm. This research will give you a better idea of the different options that are available and help you narrow down your choices.

You also want to look at the previous clients that you have worked with. Who were the most profitable and easy-going clients to work with? What were the problems that they were looking for you to solve?

This should help you in your decision-making process because what we don't want are clients that pay us big bucks, but they give us big headaches. Finding that happy medium is the way to go.

If you are in the phase where you're researching your niche market, there's several different ways to do that research. You can talk to potential clients. Often, when people are in the industry research phase of their business, they will hold free calls.

The prospect looks at it as a great opportunity to talk to a professional service provider, but the professional service provider should be taking notes, possibly even transcribing the call so that they have a good amount of data of what the true problems of various niche markets are.

You also want to look at industry trends and explore data from law firm directories. This can give you a good understanding of who your target market is and what exactly they are looking for. Attend industry events and trade shows. Most likely whatever legal software you're using, they have some type of trade show, or they will be vending at some type of legal event over the year.

I usually recommend attending at least two to three live events a year. It's a great way to network and learn about the latest trends. Since technology is evolving so rapidly, you want to make sure that the problem that you solve cannot be replaced by technology.

Your expertise needs to be valued by the clients that you plan to serve. You can also look at online forums, groups, blogs, and podcasts. These all provide you with additional research and data for your niche market.

Once you've done your research, it's time to start planning your marketing strategy. This should include everything from your web design to the way that you communicate with potential clients. When we are thinking of how we will create our marketing plan, you must ask yourself, are you looking to build brand awareness or are you looking to generate leads?

The various methods include traditional advertising like print and online ads, or more modern techniques like SEO or content marketing. Once you know what your goals are, you can start to develop a budget and create a timeline for your campaign.

Don't forget to measure those results so that you can adjust your plan as needed. With a little effort, you could create a plan that will make sure that your business succeeds.

CREATING A SALES FUNNEL

I have spent a large amount of time learning the different types of sales funnels and exactly how to create a simple funnel that works for generating leads that convert into clients.

First, let's answer the question, "What is a sales funnel? It's an essential part of any law firm's online marketing strategy. Picture what a funnel looks like. It's large at the top and gets smaller and smaller as you get near the bottom. That is essentially what you are doing with leads.

You have a large audience and then you are targeting them and creating a traffic flow to where they go down to the bottom of the funnel until they become a client. By sending targeted traffic to a specially designed landing page, law firms can easily convert leads into clients.

I love a good eBook funnel. It has worked for me and has worked for many of my clients. If you want to create your own eBook funnel, choose an eBook that is relevant to your target audience. If you do family law, and you specialize in divorce, you could create an eBook about seven things to consider before filing for divorce.

By downloading this eBook, people are helping to pre-qualify themselves as someone that is considering a divorce. You will likely have to investigate where they are in their timeline.

The eBook should have a compelling headline and a landing page that will encourage visitors to take action to download the eBook. It doesn't capture my attention if your eBook title is "All About Divorce." When you include a number, like seven (I love the number seven, it's just a lucky number!) In the title of the book, you make it clear that you're giving tips for people to easily digest.

When creating eBooks, it is very important that you point out to your audience that you know what people have tried to do on their own and the mistakes that they make. My eBook is 'Seven Financial Mistakes that Law Firm Owners Make'. This eBook has done well over the past year.

Think of a title like that as it pertains to your law firm, like 'Seven Mistakes People Make While Filing Divorce on Their Own'. When someone reads that, they'll realize maybe it is worth hiring an attorney because the cost of a mistake of doing it on their own is worse than the cost of paying an attorney.

You don't want to give them a 40- or 50-page eBook. Your eBook could be seven to ten PDF pages. Your goals it to communicate that you are the industry leader they should work with, and that you know what you're talking about.

Now that we have a good eBook and a good landing page, it's time to promote the eBook. The eBook should be on the cover of your firm's website and promoted on all your social media channels.

Make sure once they download that eBook, that they get a series of emails that will convert prospects to clients. This series of emails is called a drip campaign. You're dripping out content. You're dripping out your story. You're dripping out reasons why they should work with you.

And as you know, it often takes multiple touches to convert someone from a lead to an actual client.

When it comes to promoting this on social media, it's very easy. Let's say that you have seven tips in your book. Each one of those tips will then be a theme for a week on your social media calendar. From that theme, you will create static posts. You can create Instagram Reels and TikTok videos. You can create a blog on your website that'll boost your SEO.

For the next seven weeks, you have the focus for the content that you will produce, and all of this will reroute back to the eBook. Once they have downloaded the eBook, you now have their name, their email, and possibly their phone number. It's important to make sure that you follow up on leads weekly.

Set a goal to call at least 10 people if you do not have the consultations already booked on your calendar. Following these simple steps will help you generate more leads and grow your law firm.

HOW TO STAY FOCUSED ON YOUR NICHE MARKET

When you follow this formula, I want to warn you that you may start to get discouraged, especially after the first 30 days. You may not see the money coming in yet.

I'm here to help you with tips to stay focused on your niche market.

First, make sure you keep your marketing efforts targeted. Do not waste time and money on strategies that do not reach your target audience. Don't waste your time doing podcast interviews, creating live videos, or doing Clubhouse rooms with people that are not speaking to your specific target audience.

If you are an IP attorney who specializes in patents, you're not going to be focused on having discussions about divorce. That is not your target audience. Make sure that you keep your marketing efforts targeted. This will help you move things along faster as far as growing the audience you want to work with potential clients.

Next, stay up to date on industry trends. You need to know what is happening in your niche. This will help you adjust your marketing plan and keep your law firm ahead of the curve. As different laws are passed or you notice trends changing, you can be the one to let your audience know ahead of your competition.

They will view you as a thought leader in this industry. When you present new information to people, you make them consider working with you even quicker, because everyone has a little bit of doubt. By presenting new information, you're slowly, but surely, crushing that doubt.

The last tip is to know your competitors. Look at what other law firms in your niche are doing so you can identify areas where you are going above and beyond and areas where you can improve. Note that the strategies your competition is using do not always align with what makes sense for your marketing plan. That is perfectly fine.

You want to make sure that you have a conversation with whoever is responsible for your marketing strategy to ensure that you are reaching your target audience and that you are the number one choice ahead of your competitors.

NEXT STEPS

Now you understand that it is possible to create systems and leverage business strategies to build the law firm of your dreams.

I know this can seem like a lot of information and is probably a little overwhelming. I recommend you go back to the Table of Contents and rank the chapters in order of what would give you the most benefit.

In 90% of cases, I'd put the "Create SOPs" at the very top. It's the cornerstone of everything. There is no question that this process works - it's already worked for hundreds of firms.

If you want to talk to me personally about helping you create a plan to take your firm to the next level, email me at jayden@prestigeaccountants.com.

If you find anything in this book that I failed to explain fully, or left out a small detail that you need, I want to know. Every time we've done these things in the past, we are the ones doing the work, so it's hard to know what issues will arrive. If you run into problems at any point, just email me and I'll be happy to help.

Thank you for reading this book, and congratulations on taking your next step to reaching new heights and booking more flights!

ABOUT THE AUTHOR

Jayden Doyé

Website: https://www.prestigeaccountants.com

Podcast: https://lawandquarter.com

Jayden was not always the financial guru that he is today. Growing up in a household just shy of the federal poverty line in Prince George's County, Maryland, he knew the importance of money management but didn't have the tools to create the financial stability he so desperately craved. After graduating Towson University with a B.S in

Accounting and incurring a large amount of debt, Jayden was determined to make a change.

With a little hard work and A LOT of sacrifice, Jayden became independent, gained professional growth as an accountant at a small CPA firm in Atlanta, and became a Certified Public Accountant. Over the next years, he's worked with clients in just about every industry — helping them not only expand their financial portfolios, but to create plans that ensure financial sustainability and minimize taxability.

As a CPA, Jayden's goal is to help entrepreneurs like himself gain independence and create a unique action plan to bring more to their bottom line while paying less in taxes. Invest in yourself and start working with Jayden TODAY!

Made in the USA
Monee, IL
04 November 2026

67375731R00089